High Heaton
Cochrane Park
Benton

Alan Morgan

Tyne
Bridge
Publishing

ISBN: 978-1-739223311

Published by:

City of Newcastle Upon Tyne
Newcastle Libraries
Tyne Bridge Publishing, 2023
unless otherwise indicated
Layout design: Derek Tree

The author and publisher would like to thank Kevin Mochrie for his work on the Heaton Stannington section.

Front Cover: *This long line of what looks like similar commercial vehicles appears to be at the lower end of Newton Road, probably waiting for the signal to turn left into Stephenson Road and take part in the cavalcade of motor vehicles to celebrate the opening of the new Coast Road in October 1927. No information is given on the original photograph but the trees in the background resemble the Spinney. In fact the 'mound' can just be seen to the left and within the trees, as it remains today. Also, the haystacks indicate an autumnal time of year.*

Contents

High Heaton

Cochrane Park

Benton

High Heaton

Introduction

The area now known as High Heaton appears to have been first enclosed 'with neatly divided fields' shortly before 1785 after centuries of open moorland pasture alongside some medieval farming using the rig and furrow method of ploughing. Some of today's parkland close to the edge of Paddy Freeman's sports field with Freeman Road contains evidence of that type of farming, which is most noticeable following heavy rain or a light covering of snow when the corrugated effect is revealed. High Heaton's farm buildings, later occupied by the Freeman family, are clearly marked on a map dated 1745.

Before the 1780s there would also be evidence of coal mining left by the Heaton Banks colliery that closed in 1745. Alongside the Ouseburn there were cornmills dating from a much earlier period and the Busy Cottage ironworks became significant from around the mid-1700s.

Following the end of coal mining in Heaton and High Heaton during the 1850s, Sir William Armstrong bought the land from the Ridley family, formerly of Heaton Hall, in 1862 and leased it back to the two major farms in the area: High Laws in the north and High Heaton adjoining it further south.

In the south west part of High Heaton, adjacent to the Ouseburn Valley, several substantial villas were built during the late Victorian and early Edwardian periods and named, confusingly, the Jesmond Park Estate, probably because High Heaton did not exist at this time, whereas neighbouring Jesmond was already a well-established and popular suburb.

During the 1920s and later, the remainder of High Heaton was transformed into a suburban environment with large residential estates, schools, churches, a library and a couple of factories. A popular football club also settled on the site of a former stone quarry. The years after World War II saw the creation of a large complex of government offices as well as, a little later, a large hospital that has since gained an international reputation for organ transplants.

The approximate boundary of High Heaton used for the purposes of this book is Jesmond Dene (west), the Coxlodge waggonway (north), Benton Road (east) and Stephenson Road (south). Other identifiable places on this 1932 aerial photo include the Spinney, surrounded by housing, then clockwise around the periphery are Heaton Secondary School, Paddy Freeman's farmhouse and park, Newton Quarry, farmland, Cragside, Byker and Heaton Cemetery and parts of North Heaton.

An aerial view of High Heaton taken around 1932 which clearly shows the layout of the new estate centred around the Spinney, as well as other recognisable features of the area.

Stephenson Road

In 1965 this was the view along Stephenson Road towards the Corner House junction from the Benton Road/Coast Road roundabout before work began to extend the Coast Road dual carriageway towards the city centre. The second photograph features the garage at the corner of Chillingham Road (left) and Stephenson Road (right) with three expensive looking cars on show in 1947. Note the tramlines in the foreground, soon to be removed as trolley buses gradually replaced tramcars.

Construction work involved the demolition of the corner garage, nearly twenty shops, several houses and a Masonic Temple, recognisable in this photograph as a box-shaped building to the right of centre. Some houses on the other side of Stephenson Road also needed to be removed. The scheme, which was completed in 1967, included an underpass for Coast Road traffic as well as a system of pedestrian tunnels where a commemorative plaque was later unveiled.

The buildings on Stephenson Road appear to have been commenced immediately prior to the First World War and completed in the mid-1920s. The road was named after Sir William Haswell Stephenson (1836-1918) a local industrialist, generous benefactor to Newcastle and mayor of the city seven times. In 1900 he received a knighthood for services to Newcastle.

Stephenson Road in 1965.

Sir William Haswell Stephenson.

The garage at the corner of Chillingham Road (left) and Stephenson Road (right) in 1947 which was later demolished.

Stephenson Road in 1921 from the Benton Road/Chillingham Road junction and a few years before the Coast Road was created in 1927.

The shops on Stephenson Road in 1965.

Benton Road

Featured on this 1947 photograph is an E type tramcar about to leave a stop at the foot of Benton Road for either a terminus at Swarland Avenue or beyond to Forest Hall. Other varieties of trams existed but the livery of them all was dark maroon with cream and yellow trimmings. In 1948 trams on this route were replaced by the larger and much quieter trolley buses, whose livery was a distinctive yellow with cream and maroon trimmings. From 1966 the more manoeuvrable motor buses were introduced, whose initial colours were similar to those of the trolley buses.

The shops behind the tram are dated 1927 (date above a door lintel). 20 years later they included a butcher, baker, fishmonger, barber, confectioner and a shoe repairer. Today the same shops are occupied by a fast-food outlet, an off licence and a funeral director next to a business retailing floral tributes – very handy for Byker and Heaton cemetery, almost opposite on the other side of Benton Road.

One of the very few buildings in this part of High Heaton until the 1920s was the Blue House that stood at what is now the north east corner of the Benton Road/Coast Road junction. The building probably dated from the 18th century and most likely had been one of several toll booths controlling the approaches to Newcastle. A blacksmith occupied the premises for around 30 years from the 1840s and the last occupant before the buildings were removed for road improvements in the 1920s was a road haulage business named Speed Ltd, as pictured on the 1921 photograph. Byker and Heaton cemetery lay behind the trees.

A trolleybus on Benton Road, c1951. The marks of the tram tracks are still visible.
Photo I.C. Gumm.

An E type tramcar about to leave a stop at the foot of Benton Road in 1947.

The bottom of Benton Road in 1921 before the road improvements later that decade.

The north end of Benton Road, near Four Lane Ends in 1977.

High Heaton Estate

The High Heaton council housing estate, bounded by Cragside, Benton Road, Stephenson Road and Newton Road, covering around 75 acres was part of a much larger area of farmland acquired by Newcastle City Council from Lord Armstrong in 1920 for the purpose of building council and private housing as well as a proposed secondary school. For many years previously the land had been leased to High Heaton Farm.

Construction of the estate was in the form of a semicircle of streets radiating around the Spinney open area where the Heaton High Pit had operated until its closure in 1827. R.G. Roberts, later to become Newcastle's first official City Architect, designed the homes using an interesting variety of materials and styles in the 'garden suburb' tradition that included three-four-and five-roomed dwellings. Building began in 1925 and continued during the following year. Eventually, nearly 900 homes with gardens were built in about 20 thoroughfares, each named after parts of Northumberland associated with Lord Armstrong. The estate also contained a few sites for garden allotments.

This aerial photograph below, taken around the early 1930s, highlights the new streets surrounding the Spinney, in front of which is the square wooden school for infants that later became High Heaton's first public library. Close to the school on Newton Road are some of the estate's new shops. Other shops were situated at the corner of Benton Road and Stephenson Road. The second photograph features part of Plessey Terrace under construction in 1926.

The High Heaton Estate in about 1930.

Plessey Terrace under construction in 1926. Just one of the many streets in the High Heaton Estate.

Byker and Heaton Cemetery

As Byker and Heaton expanded in the late nineteenth century, residents began to campaign for a burial ground nearer their homes, rather than having to use the inconvenient and expensive All Saints Cemetery in Jesmond Road, originally intended for those living in the parish of All Saints.

Eventually a 12-acre field was secured by Newcastle Council at a time when the area now known as High Heaton was almost all farmers' fields. The chosen site adjoined Benton Lane (now Benton Road) which connected with what became Heaton Road and Chillingham Road, making travelling more convenient. Opening as a municipal cemetery in 1890, it followed the practice of dividing the land by a central carriageway. The area north of the carriageway was reserved for members of the Church of England, while other denominations were interred to the south. Each side had a separate chapel. In 1913 the cemetery was doubled in size following the purchase of land previously belonging to the adjoining Benton Park/Red Hall private estate. Two years later a Jewish section was created within this extension.

Notable interments include Private Edward Lawson who was awarded the V.C. in 1897 as a result of his bravery while rescuing fellow soldiers under heavy gunfire on India's North West frontier with Afghanistan. One of the most striking monuments covers the vault of the Risi family, Italian immigrants who set up a local ice cream manufacturing business in 1899 and continue to be involved in the catering trade.

This recent photograph shows both chapels near the entrance to the cemetery on Benton Road.

Byker and Heaton Cemetery in 2023.

Cremona Park Garden Toffery

Albert S Wilkin (1883-1943), the son of a Cumbrian policeman, moved to Sunderland in 1904 to become a grocer's apprentice and after a few more years opened his own toffee-making business in a nearby disused chapel. Wilkin adopted the well-known 'Red Boy' painting (by Sir Thomas Lawrence of seven-year-old Charles William Lambton) to decorate his tins of toffee. By 1918 they had become a national brand and needed larger premises.

In 1920 the business, now known as A.S. Wilkin Ltd., transferred to a 12-acre site alongside Benton Road, Newcastle, previously occupied by the Royal Flying Corps. The new factory buildings were spacious, airy and spotless with up-to-date machinery. Anyone could inspect every part of the works without notice. Most of the employees were women who wore overalls and caps in fawn and blue. Outside the factory were large gardens with fruit trees, shrubs and flowers, looked after by several gardeners, along with tennis courts, basketball grounds and hockey pitches. Later known as Cremona Park, it was claimed to be the world's only Garden Toffery where toffee, and nothing but toffee, was manufactured under ideal and hygienic conditions in the perfect setting of beautiful gardens.

Wilkin was one of the most active promoters of the North East Coast Exhibition of Industry, Science and Art at Newcastle's Exhibition Park in 1929, where he presented a championship cup for wrestling. A decade later Wilkin was knighted for services to industry, largely as a result of his major involvement in the formation of the Northern Industrial Developments Organisation that led to the establishment of the Team Valley Trading Estate at Gateshead in 1936 with the objective of alleviating high unemployment.

Around 20 years after Wilkin's death in 1943 the business was taken over by the Rowntree Mackintosh Group and closed a year or two later. Most of the site today is occupied by Sainsbury's supermarket and a car showroom and workshop.

At the centre of this 1938 aerial photograph is the Garden Toffery with its tall chimney and spacious grounds to the rear. In the top half of the photograph are the Cochrane Park residential estate and the adjacent cemetery with part of the High Heaton estate below.

Photo Credit: Historic Environment Scotland.

Cremona Toffee Works at Cremona Park in 1938. Inset: Inside the factory and (right) an advert for their famous toffee.

Riddell Collection.

The A.S. Wilkin factory at Cremona Park in 1938 had state-of-the-art facilities. Inset: One the company's delivery vans.

Riddell Collection.

An A.S. Wilkin Ltd staff outing in 1938.

Sylvan Jam Factory

Apparently, it was the wife of entrepreneur John Smith who first suggested to her husband that the time had probably arrived for them to consider opening a business making jams, preserves, pickles and chutney. Mrs Smith had already developed recipes for these products that had impressed family and friends. She also had a quantity of gooseberries that she did not wish to see wasted.

The Sylvan Manufacturing Co. Ltd., locally known as the Jam Factory opened in the mid-1920s, alongside the Cremona Park Toffery at Benton Road, immediately prior to the development of High Heaton as it is today. It was often possible to tell which fruit was being processed on a particular day. John Smith's method was to buy an entire crop then send his girls to pick the fruit, which could be anywhere in Britain and sometimes Europe. The business prospered for many years, with orders coming from as far away as Iceland.

From the mid-1950s the premises were occupied by the CWS Buildings department then an engineering centre for the Post Office. The original buildings were demolished at a later date and today the site is covered by a car showroom and workshop between Sainsbury's supermarket and a gym/fitness centre.

In this aerial view dated 1938 the factory is sandwiched between the much larger Cremona Park Toffee works (centre) and the Greystones residential estate, alongside the former Coxlodge Waggonway at the top of the photograph.

Benton Road in 1977 showing a very small part of the factory to the extreme right of the photograph.

Photo Credit: Historic Environment Scotland.

The 'Jam Factory' in Benton Road, 1938, located in between the larger Cremona works and the Greystones residential estate.

Benton Pit

The site of the Benton pit is now covered by part of the 1930s Greystones residential estate, close to where the Coxlodge waggonway crossed what is now Benton Road. Originally belonging to Longbenton Colliery, the pit was forced to close in 1766 because of serious flooding but ironically was able to reopen around 50 years later, having inadvertently contributed to the flooding of neighbouring pits, including the Heaton High Pit, belonging to the Heaton Main colliery, and the loss of so many lives in the pit disaster of 1815. A colliery is a collective term for any number of pits owned by the colliery.

At this point Heaton Main colliery took over the now water-free Benton pit and renamed it the Howard Main pit, after the Earl of Carlisle of Castle Howard in North Yorkshire, who owned the mineral rights. Following a few years of indifferent production, in 1825 the colliery owners decided to sink another pit on an adjacent site, which they called the New Pit.

Following a major reorganisation of the Heaton Main colliery in 1836, the Heaton High and Benton pits appear to have been worked together with Bigge's Main colliery at Wallsend and six years later their combined workforce was 491. 176 were surface workers with 315 working underground, including 108 hewers and around 120 teenage boys who operated ventilation doors, pushed tubs of coal or guided horses around underground waggonways on shifts normally lasting 12 hours. Most of these workers, it is thought, lived at Bigge's Main village, Wallsend.

One 13-year-old boy who lived nearly three miles away at Ouseburn walked to the pit for the start of his 4am shift, worked for 12 hours driving horses, returned home by 5pm for a dinner of potatoes and meat then washed and went to bed with no time for recreation. Some boys worked a continuous double shift of 24 hours or even longer, saying that they preferred underground employment because it was warmer in winter. Among the more elderly miners was a 77-year-old who had toiled for 70 years as a miner and a 93-year-old who had worked until the age of 85.

The two pits at Benton closed in 1852 due to flooding following the demise of the Friar's Goose colliery in Gateshead and its powerful pumping engine that had assisted other pits in the Tyne basin to avoid flooding. The 60-year life of the Heaton Main colliery with its pits in the Heaton and High Heaton areas was now at an end. The attached map (c1860) indicates the site of the Benton pit in relation to the waggonway, Benton Lane (Road) and Heaton High Pit.

Opposite: A map from around 1860 shows the position of the Benton pit and, below, a 1938 aerial view showing the pit in the background.

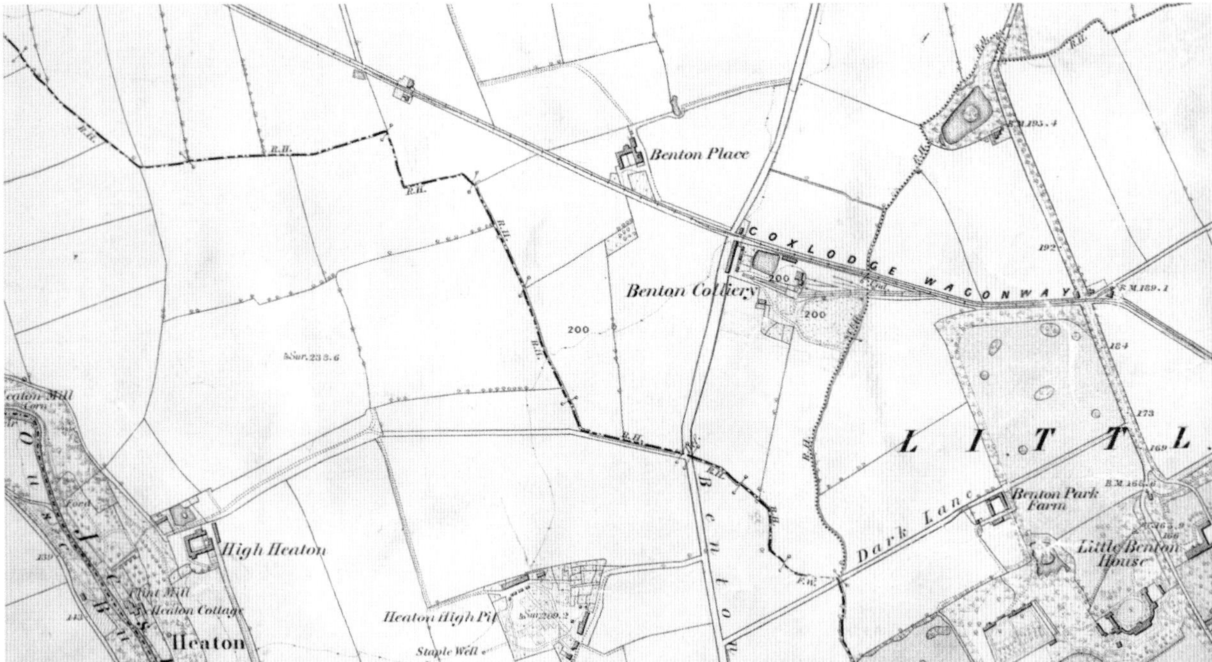
Benton Place
COXLODGE WAGONWAY
Benton Colliery
200
L I T T L
Benton Park Farm
Dark Lane
Little Benton House
High Heaton
Heaton High Pit
Staple Well
Heaton Cottage
Heaton

Benton Pit

Coxlodge Waggonway

The Brandling family of Gosforth opened the Coxlodge Waggonway in 1808 as part of their plan to increase the size of their colliery at Coxlodge by the addition of the Jubilee pit (1809) and the Regent pit (1812). At nearly five miles long, the waggonway began at East Kenton and ran almost in a direct line via Coxlodge, Gosforth and High Heaton to riverside staiths at Wallsend. This longer route was preferred to the shorter and more obvious line to the river in order to avoid the expense and delay of having to use keel boats.

Initially waggons laden with coal were pulled by horses on wooden rails. After a few years George Stephenson, a friend of the Brandlings, converted the entire track to iron rails, enabling 'travelling engines' to operate instead of horses that were becoming expensive to acquire and maintain. Early locomotives could pull waggons full of coal at speeds of up to three and a half miles per hour. Until the waggonway closed in 1884, following a change in ownership, it also served the collieries at Fawdon, Gosforth and Heaton.

After nearly 20 years of neglect, that part of the original waggonway between Gosforth and the Wallsend boundary was converted by the newly formed Tyneside Tramways and Tramroads Company into a standard gauge electric tramway with extensions at each end, either to Gosforth Park Gates or North Shields. The formal opening took place in 1902, performed by Mrs Watson-Armstrong. At just over 11 miles long, open top double-deck trams covered the distance in around 50 minutes with a 10-minute frequency of service. Ordinary passengers paid 1d per mile, while workers paid 1/2d. The company's livery was predominantly dark green with some cream and each tram could be rapidly converted into a totally enclosed lower deck during wintry conditions.

The tram served large numbers of workers travelling to and from the riverside industries and an all-night service for miners, known as the 'pitman's special' also operated between collieries near the Gosforth Park tram terminus and Haddrick's Mill Bridge.

In 1913 a serious accident occurred when two trams, each travelling at around 10mph, collided head on in dense fog between two loops in the single track alongside what was then the Benton Park golf course. Two people died and another five were injured.

Due to the growing number of local bus services and the high cost of renewing the trams and track, the line closed in 1930 and the track was lifted. A pedestrian and cycleway, known locally as the 'tram track' was developed between South Gosforth and Wallsend. In recent years it has been resurfaced and improved.

This superb sketch of Gosforth colliery around 1840 by Thomas Hair shows both bridges over the Ouseburn near Haddrick's Mill. A horse and cart can be seen crossing the lower stone bridge (still there) while over the higher viaduct-cum-waggonway (demolished) a group of coal waggons is about to be hauled up a gradient by an out-of-sight stationary steam engine at the South Gosforth end of today's tram track. Information panels are positioned near the Coach Lane crossing and close to St Francis Church.

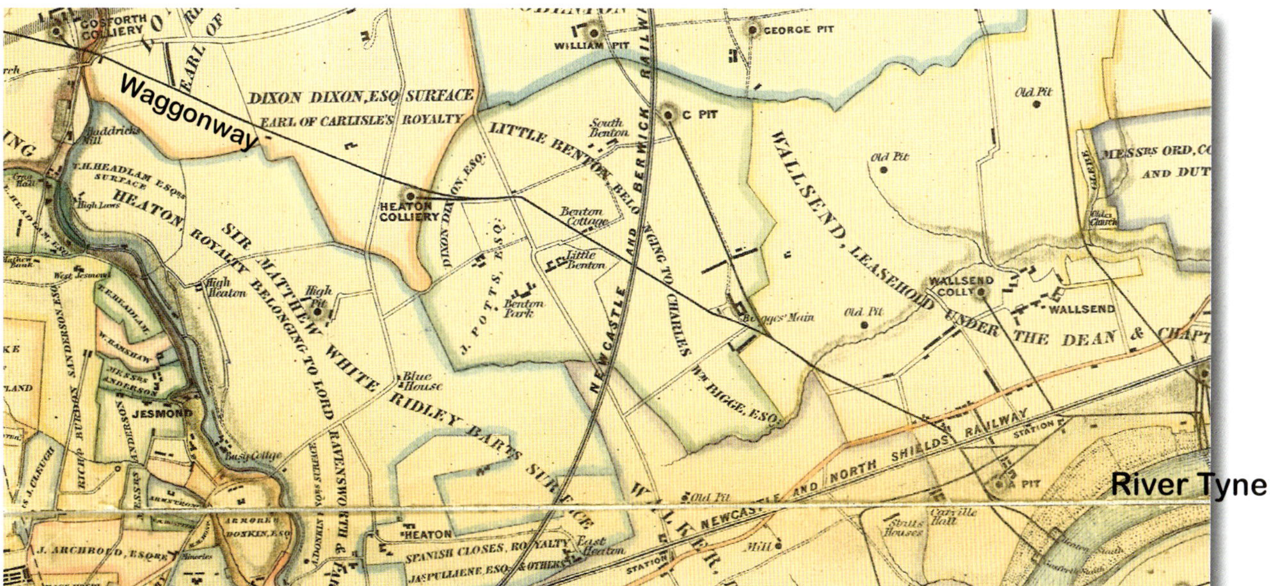

Bell's 1861 Map of the Coal District, showing the route of the waggonway. Top right: The waggonway today is used as popular walking and cycling route. Top left: Thomas Hair's Sketch of Gosforth colliery c1840.

Newton Park Hotel

The Newton Park Hotel, pictured here in 1949, remains as High Heaton's only pub. It opened shortly after the outbreak of World War Two, facing Benton Road alongside the former Coxlodge waggonway and at the edge of a residential estate.

Built of brick in the neo-Tudor style, with tall ornamental chimneys, it also features the distinctive flat Tudor arch over each of the main entrance doors. The building has been altered and extended over the decades. At present it is managed by a Suffolk-based brewery.

The tramlines in the road disappeared during the 1950s, a few years after tramcars on this route were replaced by trolley buses.

Riddell Collection.

Inside the Newton Park Hotel in 1949, High Heaton's only pub.

St Francis Parish Church

St Gabriel's Church on Heaton Road served as the parish church for the emerging suburb of High Heaton until 1935 when a temporary timber mission church-cum-church hall was provided at Cragside to serve this far-flung corner of the parish. At that time Cragside formed part of the city boundary and was also the terminus for trams approaching from Newcastle city centre along what is now called Benton Road. The building (still there) cost around £1,350 was fitted with furnishings largely recycled from St Peter's Church in Ellison Place (about to be demolished) along with an organ from St Gabriel's former church hall on Chillingham Road.

Increased congregations and plans for parish status highlighted the urgent need for a permanent and larger church building, which in turn brought about a generous donation of land from Lord Armstrong alongside the tram track near the north end of Cleveland Gardens. The arrangement seemed ideal at the time because of its proposed location at the centre of a parish expected to expand. However, this growth never took place because in 1946 the farmland north of the tram track, originally intended for housing was compulsorily purchased by the Government to build the extensive Ministry of Pensions and National Insurance complex as required by the new National Health Service about to be introduced two years later. The outcome of this situation plus the scrapping of plans to replace the tram track with a road resulted in the church buildings remaining isolated at the northern edge of the parish. Once the collapse of the road scheme had been confirmed, the main entrance of the vicarage, originally facing the tram track, was moved to the opposite side of the building.

Work began on the new church in 1952. Post-war building restrictions resulted in a plain brick building. The consecration ceremony was held on 3 October 1953, the anniversary of the death of St Francis of Assisi in 1226. This early photograph of the church as viewed from Cleveland Gardens is dated 1957, the year when the adjacent vicarage was completed. The church hall opened in 1978. The former mission church at Cragside, pictured opposite in 1966, continued in use as a base for the church's Scout and associated groups.

The original structure of St Francis Parish Church in Cragside, in 1966.

Newton Road

The smartly dressed gentleman featured on this 1909 photograph is almost certainly an official from Newcastle City Council inspecting the appalling road conditions at the north end of what was then called Newton Road, near Haddricks Mill bridge over the Ouseburn. Around this time there had been proposals to extend the city's boundary in this area and it would appear that this official had been chauffeured here in the adjacent car BB55, which must have been one of the earliest registered vehicles in Newcastle, probably belonging to the council.

Newton Road was named after Sir Henry William Newton (1842-1914), the locally born physician and alderman who served twice as Newcastle's mayor and was councillor for All Saints ward for 48 years. The road, nearly one and a half miles long was formed around 1883, at a cost of nearly £4000 to connect Heaton with South Gosforth and its colliery. Around 1928, that part of the road between the entrance to Paddy Freeman's Park and South Gosforth was renamed Freeman Road after the well-known High Heaton farming family called Freeman.

Also in the photograph are the roof tops (very faint) of some of the early houses in Lilburn Gardens, along with Bridge Row to the left, a short terrace of eight cottages. At the 1881 census these cottages housed 40 people. Virtually all the male inhabitants were colliery workers, presumably at the nearby South Gosforth pit, which closed a few years later. Shortly after 1909 the cottages were demolished, partly to make way for the construction of Lartington Gardens.

Torday Collection.

Newton Road Shops, outside of Heaton Stannington Football Club, c1965. Inset: Sir Henry William Newton

Freeman Hospital

Prince Charles officially opened the Freeman Hospital in May 1978. The Freeman absorbed several smaller hospitals on a 35-acre greenfield site with over 800 beds and 18 operating theatres.

The new hospital cost around £15m and was named after Freeman Road. The foundation stone was laid in 1972 by Sir Keith Joseph, Secretary of State for Social Services. Five years later the first patient signed the official visitors' book and was given a glass of champagne.

Although the plans for a new hospital were initially opposed by some doctors because of the possible duplication of medical services already available at other hospitals in the city, the Freeman Hospital became one of the most technologically advanced in Europe and a national leader in the field of organ transplants. The first successful heart transplant at the Freeman took place in 1985. Two years later came the first successful heart transplant for a child in the UK and the first successful single lung transplant in Europe. In 1990 the Freeman performed Europe's first successful double lung transplant, gaining an international reputation for this type of surgery.

Photos: Tom Yellowley

The Institute of Transplantation, Freeman Hospital, Freeman Road, 2011, and, right, Maggie's Newcastle Cancer Care Centre, 2013, which is also at the site.

This aerial view from 1976, taken two years before the official opening, shows the Freeman hospital site framed by Freeman Road (top), Daylesford Drive Estate (right), the Coxlodge Waggonway (bottom) and Melville Grove (left).

Paddy Freeman's Park

Paddy Freeman's Park in 1906 and, below, in the 1960s. The park was originally a small part of a much larger area of agricultural land farmed for several decades by the Freeman family and as tenants initially of the Ridley's of Heaton Hall and then Sir William Armstrong from the late 1860s.

Torday Collection.

The park in the late 1960s and, bottom right, as it looks today

Torday Collection.

St George's United Reformed Church

St George's Presbyterian Church, as it was originally known, opened in 1938 at the corner of Newton Road and Boundary Gardens alongside the church hall, completed six years earlier. Built to seat 350, the total cost of the church amounted to £5260, excluding the land which, together with the church hall, had been gifted by the Presbytery. The church had moved from its previous location at Jesmond Road because it was felt it would benefit by being situated in the rapidly expanding new suburb of High Heaton. Following the amalgamation in 1972 of the Presbyterian and Congregational churches in England and Wales, it was renamed St George's United Reformed Church.

Before construction work began in around 1937, church members were involved in removing over 20 trees from the site. They were remnants of a line once bordering the north side of Newton Road, probably planted to screen the adjacent stone quarry, now a football ground. Apparently, it was then the job of the church's Rover Scouts to dig out the stumps and saw all the timber into logs for sale.

Since the 1700s Tyneside, because of its diverse industry, had been a popular destination for the 'poor and industrious adventurers from Scotland', which probably explains why Presbyterianism became the most widespread of the non-conformist sects in the area for so many years. The earliest of their meeting houses in Newcastle had been in the Sandgate, Castle Garth and Silver Street districts, where vacant premises were often converted to accommodate large numbers of people, in some cases up to 800 in one building. Later their places of worship spread to the upper part of the town and eventually into the suburbs.

A recent photograph of St George's United Reformed Church.

Heaton Stannington Football Club

The earliest reference to Heaton Stannington Football Club appears in the 1903/04 season, when the team finished fifth in the Newcastle and District Amateur League (Division Two). They played alongside Miller's Lane, now the Fossway. In 1904, they resigned from the league and there is no further mention of the club until 1910 suggesting that they had folded and reformed.

The Stannington part of the club's name appears to refer to the small village adjacent to the Blagdon Estate, near Morpeth, that still belongs to the Ridley family. For many years the Ridleys owned land in Heaton and lived at the now demolished Heaton Hall. Some of the surrounding streets are Stannington Avenue, Stannington Grove and Stannington Place. It is thought that either the original club secretary or perhaps a majority of players originated from around these streets.

By 1913 the club's home games were taking place at Paddy Freeman's Park in High Heaton and by the 1930s they were playing on pitches alongside the recently opened Coast Road, a site now occupied by Ravenswood School. In 1934 they won the Tynemouth Infirmary Minor Cup, the club's first trophy.

In 1935 the club rented a recently infilled former stone quarry at the top end of Newton Road from Lord Armstrong. They called it Newton Park. In 1936/37 they became Northern Amateur League Division One champions, won the Northumberland FA Amateur Cup and were runners-up in the Northern Amateur League Challenge Cup. This 1938 image features the club (white shirts) in action against Bishop Auckland during the first round of the FA Amateur Cup, which they won 3-2.

During the Second World War, when football was suspended, the ground was occupied by the military and in 1940 enemy bombs intended for this army compound missed their target and caused serious damage to property in nearby Cleveland Gardens.

Following the end of hostilities, the club re-joined the Northern League in 1946, but resigned in 1952. In 1972 they stepped up to the influential Wearside League, but were forced to resign a decade later because of a large increase in rent by the club trustees. Around this time there were plans to convert the ground into a supermarket, but it was saved by a High Court ruling.

Known by supporters as the 'Stan,' the club now play in black and white striped shirts with black shorts and socks. A new club house opened in 1999, followed in 2006 by new changing rooms. In 2007 the 2,000-capacity ground was renamed Grounsell Park in memory of Bob Grounsell, a former player and revered club official. Floodlighting was installed in 2013 and in the following year a new 50-seater stand was erected with another 50-seater stand following in January 2022. The club rejoined the Northern League in 2013 and were promoted to Division 1 in 2022.

Heaton Stannnington beat Bishop Auckland 3-2 in the first round of the English FA Amateur Cup on 15 January 1938.

The Heaton Stannington line-up of September 1953: Front Row (left to right), Jardine, Hall, Simpson, Muir and Cutter. Back Row (left to right), Whitfield, Newby, Stewart, Proud, Drummond and Grounsell.

Photos: Carys Street.

Heaton Stannington Football Club as it looks in 2023

Heaton Pig Club

There were several pig clubs in Newcastle during the Second World War, established in an attempt to ease the problems caused by food rationing, which did not end until around the mid-1950s, nearly a decade after the conclusion of hostilities. One of these clubs was in High Heaton on undeveloped land, now part of the Patterdale Gardens/Mitcham Crescent area. The animals were fed and fattened on kitchen waste. The photograph is undated but thought to be from around the 1950s.

Although vegetables and fruit were never rationed during the war, the Government began a 'Dig for Victory' campaign to supplement rationed foods and promote healthy eating. One of the garden allotment areas was close to the pig club where the author, as a young teenager, grew vegetables for family consumption as well as to qualify for the Boy Scouts gardening badge. Unfortunately there are few, if any, photographs of this activity due to the scarcity of film at the time.

Second World War bomb damage at Cleveland Gardens. The bomb just missed the football ground, which at the time was a military compound with searchlight(s) and an anti-aircraft gun. Right: Posters like this one encouraged this author to grow his own vegetables.

Heaton Pig Club formed during the Second World War on undeveloped ground that was later to become Patterdale Gardens. The Pigs were kept in a variety of places and fed on kitchen waste.

Cragside Primary School

Cragside School, at the corner of Cleveland Gardens and Cragside, opened in April 1937 to receive around 300 infants and juniors, most of whom were transferred from the nearby temporary wooden school in the Spinney. However, other children were also admitted, such as those already living in High Heaton at an earlier date but required to travel elsewhere for their schooling who were at risk crossing busy roads.

There is no reference in the school's log book to any official opening of the building. This may well have been due to the turmoil caused by the abdication of King Edward VIII in December 1936 and the coronation of his younger brother King George VI in May 1937.

The school was extremely traffic conscious and encouraged road safety awareness among children by launching a new road game using miniature cars and buses. With the luxury of two assembly halls the school had the option of transforming one into a theatre for the production of plays and concerts.

The author's class of 20 seven-year-olds in March 1938 is featured on this photograph. They include Sheila Suffield, Joan Harmer, Peter Cook, Tommy Barnes. Alan Stothard, David Baker and Norman Purdy. Alan Morgan is in the middle of the back row.

During the early years of the Second World War the school was evacuated to Morpeth for several weeks until the construction of air raid shelters at Cragside was completed. Three sides of those shelters have now been removed, leaving the fourth as a barrier between the school playground and Cleveland Gardens. Notice a ventilation brick in this photograph of the wall alongside Cleveland Gardens.

Now known as Cragside Primary School, with around 400 pupils aged four to eleven, the school has a four-star rating and was considered outstanding at a recent OFSTED inspection, as recorded on this recent photograph.

The author's class of 20 seven-year-olds in March 1938 at Cragside Primary School.

Torday Collection.

Cragside Primary School yard in the 1960s

Cragside Primary School today with, inset, the ventilation brick from the former air raid shelter.

Heaton High Pit

Heaton High Pit, sometimes known as the Far Pit, opened between 1801 and 1804 on what had been farmland and prospered for nearly 25 years until serious flooding led to its closure in 1827. Mining in this northern part of the Heaton coalfield then continued at Benton, alongside the Coxlodge Waggonway, on a site almost opposite today's Newton Park pub on Benton Road, This and the remaining pits in this coalfield were collectively known as the Heaton Main Colliery. It was sunk in 1792 to mine the valuable High Main seam of coal, around six feet thick and about 500 feet below most of Heaton and High Heaton. For almost 150 years, ending in the 1860s, Heaton was at the technological forefront of world coal mining, with one of the largest coalmines in the world at one period and where most of its output was shipped to London as part of the very profitable sea-coal trade.

The only major accident at the colliery during 60 years of mining occurred in 1815 when, following exploratory borings to locate the High Main seam, the flooded workings of an adjacent abandoned colliery were unleashed. As a result, 41 men, 34 boys and 37 horses were trapped by rising water and all suffocated. In 1966 a brass memorial plaque was unveiled at the entrance to the neighbouring high-rise flats (still there) because at that time it was thought the disaster occurred beneath the Heaton High Pit area. It has since been established that this pit had been closed for repairs at the time and the tragedy happened some 300 feet beneath St Teresa's Church and Presbytery on Heaton Road, where in recent years another plaque has been fixed to a brick wall. Entry to the extensive mine workings had apparently been gained from the Engine Pit, another of the colliery's pits, now below part of Heaton Rail Junction.

The site of the Heaton High Pit, its cottages and allotments are now mostly covered by the Spinney, which is a grass covered recreational area with scattered trees. The long-held belief that each tree represented a life lost in the pit disaster has been rejected on the grounds that it was customary to plant trees on the site of any abandoned pithead.

This recent photograph taken in the Spinney features the tree-covered mound assumed to have concealed the former pit shaft that gave access to the mine and its extensive underground workings. Also in the photograph are the high-rise Spinney flats, together with High Heaton's most recent public library to the left. An information panel is situated close to the mound.

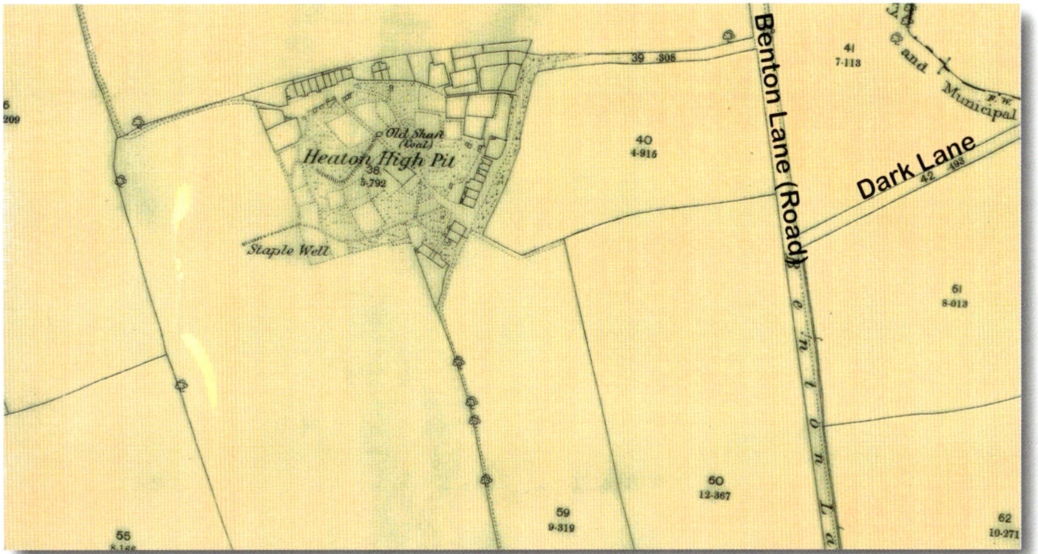

An 1858 map showing Heaton High Pit and, below, a recent photo of the Spinney featuring the mound.

Heaton High Pit Cottages

At the time of the first available census in 1841, 14 years after the Heaton High Pit closed, 26 dwellings were clustered around the pithead. 127 people lived there, of whom 39 were described as miners, probably working at the Benton New Pit, not too far away.

It was usual for mining families to be mobile in pursuit of improved pay and conditions and in 1807 hewers, the largest section of the workforce, were earning around £33 a year, a substantial wage at the time. Each miner was also entitled to rent-free accommodation and a quantity of free coal.

Most of the cottages had been removed by the time this photograph was taken in 1922. This remaining building probably contained two or three separate dwellings and was demolished a few years later. Part of Weldon Crescent now occupies the site.

An illustration from Beamish showing the working conditions of a hewer down the pit.

A remaining pit cottage in 1922 located on what is now Weldon Crescent.

Temporary Wooden Infants' School

The school opened in 1929 with an intake of 164 children, as an emergency measure to provide education for infants in a rapidly developing residential area where the nearest schools for five-year-olds were either at Tosson Terrace in North Heaton or even further away along Chillingham Road. The half-acre site chosen for the school, originally intended for an institute, was at the edge of the Spinney, almost opposite the recently opened Heaton Secondary School on Newton Road.

Designed for up to 300 children, the school consisted of six classrooms in several wooden huts arranged in three sides of a square around a yard for play. Classes of up to 50 pupils were considered acceptable at the time.

It was originally intended that the huts could be reassembled elsewhere once the permanent school had been built. However, after the temporary school closed in March 1937 the huts remained on site and became High Heaton's first public library, which opened seven months later. The huts were replaced by the new permanent library in 1967.

The children in this photograph are waving home-made Union Jacks on Empire Day in 1936, an annual event dating from the reign of Queen Victoria that celebrated her birthday on 24 May.

Children at the temporary wooden school wave home-made Union Jacks on Empire Day in 1936.

Library

High Heaton's first permanent branch library opened in 1967 on a site adjacent to the temporary wooden huts. Circular in shape, the single-storey building was designed by Williamson, Faulkner-Brown and partners, the architects who had been responsible for the prize-winning library at Jesmond, four years earlier. A special feature of the library was the partially glazed zig-zag perimeter wall that allowed as much daylight as possible to illuminate the shelves of books. Councillor Arthur Grey officially opened the library during 1968.

This 1967 photograph shows the earlier temporary library standing in front of the new permanent library and the flats built four years previously at the edge of the Spinney.

In 2008 the library was rebuilt on the same site in a more contemporary style that was equipped for the digital age. Financial cutbacks threatened closure in 2013 and today the library operates restricted opening hours.

The temporary wooden library in front of the new one in 1967. Opposite: The new library in use in 1969.

FAMOUS PEOPLE
HISTORY
OTHER COUNTRIES
REFERENCE BOOKS
EXTRA
STORY BOOKS

The interior of the 1967 library with its walls designed to let in as much light as possible.

Another new High Heaton Library was opened on the same site in 2008. Here it is in 2023.

Heaton Secondary School

Newcastle Council's first secondary school was opened in 1928 by Viscount Grey of Fallodon on a large greenfield site between Newton Road and Jesmond Park West. Described at the time as a 'noble heritage' the school consisted of two identical square two-storey buildings (one for girls and one for boys), each built around a central open area, but joined together to form a large rectangular block surrounded by playing fields. Costing £150,000 the school could accommodate up to 1,000 pupils.

Later in the year, King George V and Queen Mary visited the school where they were greeted by exercise and dance displays. This photograph shows the royal couple as they were about to leave the school for their next engagement – the opening of the Tyne Bridge.

In July 1940 enemy aircraft bombed Newcastle and the school dining room and quadrangle were damaged. The school caretaker was killed when his house, adjoining Newton Road, was wrecked.

Originally called Heaton Secondary School, the name was changed to Heaton Grammar School for Boys and Heaton High School for Girls, followed by Heaton School under the comprehensive system. In 1983, following a merger with Manor Park School at Benton due to falling pupil numbers and Government cutbacks, the school became Heaton Manor. In 2004 a new and larger building for 1,900 boys and girls replaced the out-of-date 1928 school. The school was renamed Jesmond Park Academy in 2019.

Heaton Secondary School in 1949, surrounded by Southlands (upper left) and Newton Road.

King George V and Queen Mary visited Heaton Secondary Schools on the 10th October 1928.

Riddell Collection.

Photo: Dorothy Graham.

A modern view of the school which was renamed Jesmond Park Academy in 2019. Opposite page: From 1949, Heaton Grammar School's junior football team and second XI cricket team.

Jesmond Park Estate

Any walker leaving the northern end of Armstrong Park around 1906 would probably have noticed this view of some of the substantial villas emerging on the new Jesmond Park Estate. Over a century later, trees now obscure whatever buildings remain and, due to the construction of the Cradlewell Bypass in the 1990s, the pedestrian bridge in the foreground had to be extended over a wider Benton Bank, which resulted in the demolition of North Lodge, immediately behind the bridge.

Around 1889 Lord Armstrong sold land in this area to a builder who engaged local architect Frank W. Rich to design an estate of 32 villas accessed by three roads named Barrington Gardens, Crompton Road and Melbury Road. The estate was claimed to have 'all the charms of a country estate' because of its elevation, good drainage and adjoining countryside, all within easy reach of the city centre. Each ornate individually designed villa was to have at least one third of an acre of land, between 12 and 16 rooms, stables, a lawn tennis court and possibly a greenhouse.

Barrington Gardens and Crompton Road were later renamed Jesmond Park West and Jesmond Park East respectively and it took several years for the estate to be completed, not always to the original plan. John Ferguson, the initial builder, lived in Jesmond Park East for a number of years. Other Newcastle business families living on the estate included the Bainbridges, Beavans and Fenwicks.

After 1945 a few of the larger villas were replaced with modern developments, while others were demolished for the proposed new Coast Expressway that never materialised, leaving some vacant land since converted into a small plantation with public access.

1906 view of part of the Jesmond Park Estate.

Cochrane Park

Introduction

The Cochrane Park residential estate was developed following the demolition of two eighteenth century mansions in extensive grounds, Benton Hall and Benton Park, during the early to mid 1930s. Its completion was delayed by the Second World War. The estate was named after the adjacent sports ground donated by Sir Cecil Algernon Cochrane for Armstrong College (now part of Newcastle University) where he had studied. In the 1920s Cochrane funded the construction of the Students' Union building in the University's King's Walk. His many other charitable gifts were varied and often anonymous.

Cochrane, the fourth generation of a West Midlands family of ironmasters, was born at Seghill in Northumberland and, after leaving Oxford University entered a local branch of the family business, later becoming its chairman. As one of the north's leading industrialists, he also served as a director of the Consett Ironworks and the Newcastle and Gateshead Gas Company and was on the board of several colliery companies. For a couple of years during the First World War, Cochrane represented South Shields as a Liberal M.P. and was knighted in 1933. A steam locomotive on the local Tanfield Railway is named Sir Cecil A Cochrane.

Some of the estate's street names appear to derive from locations in Britain or abroad connected with the Liddell family of Benton Park. A Liddell lived at Sherfield Manor near Reading and another lived at Martello Place in Felixtowe. Martello towers were built along England's southern and eastern coastline during the early 1800s to defend against Napoleon's threatened invasion. Longridge Avenue is almost certainly named after Longridge Towers near Berwick, the marital home of one of the Liddell daughters. St Julien may relate to an area in northern France where a great-grandson of the Liddells was possibly killed during the First World War. Warwick Hall in Cumbria is also thought to have connections with the Liddell family. Turbinia recalls the success of the world's first steam turbine-powered vessel, built at Wallsend, that became the fastest ship afloat at the Naval Review to celebrate Queen Victoria's Diamond Jubilee in 1897. The 100ft long ship is on permanent display at the Newcastle Discovery Museum.

The 1927 image shows the recently opened Coast Road heading east towards the coast with Benton Park and Benton Hall both concealed by trees on the left. The fields on the right eventually became part of the North Heaton residential estate.

Photo Credit: Historic Environment Scotland.

The Coast Road in 1927 heading east towards the coast. Inset: A rare photo of Sir Cecil Algernon Cochrane.

Coast Road

The new Coast Road between Chillingham Road and Billy Mill at North Shields was opened in October 1927 by the Minister of Transport attended by a large group of dignitaries. Following the opening ceremony near Chillingham Road, a cavalcade of 50 cars and a dozen motor buses carried officials over the 'fine concrete surface' for nearly five miles to Billy Mill for a similar ceremony. Three of the motor buses were double-decked vehicles, a new type of transport. Until then single-decked buses had been the norm.

The new road provided a direct link to the seaside resorts instead of earlier, more circuitous routes. Shortly after the opening ceremony over 3,000 daily road users were recorded. Although built as a single carriageway, land was reserved at either side for future expansion. The cost of around £217,000 was half funded by the Ministry of Transport with the remainder met by the Corporations of Newcastle, Tynemouth and Wallsend, with Longbenton UDC paying a much smaller share. At a time of high unemployment in the area, this job creation project was calculated to have saved £31,000 in dole money during each year of construction.

A major feature of the civil engineering work involved the way a new steel girder bridge had been 'rolled into position' to carry the existing main east coast railway over the new road with the minimum of disruption to road and rail traffic.

During the 1960s the Coast Road was upgraded to a three-lane dual carriageway that included the replacement of roundabout systems with underpasses for both traffic and pedestrians. There had also been significant civil engineering problems to be overcome, such as the discovery of a 200ft disused mine shaft, poor sub-soil conditions and badly fractured foundations of the earlier carriageway.

This 1927 photograph shows the cavalcade of transport as it slowly made its way beneath the railway bridge along the recently completed Coast Road towards North Shields following the opening ceremony near Chillingham Road.

Crowds gather for the opening of the Coast Road in 1927.

Former Wills Tobacco Factory

Sir Robert Sinclair, chairman of the Imperial Tobacco Company Ltd (the parent company of WD & HO Wills) opened this imposing factory on a 25-acre site in 1950. The various buildings were designed in the Art Deco style by the company's architect, Cecil Hockin, but not constructed immediately due to the outbreak of the Second World War. Built largely of red brick and Portland stone on steel frames, the works lay to the rear of the impressive administration block, whose massive central entrance tower (with clock and company name) overlooked the Coast Road, close to the East Coast main railway.

The factory's peak years were in the 1970s when the workforce of at least 1,000 produced around 20,000 cigarettes a minute, mainly Woodbine and Capstan, on a 24-hour/7-day shift pattern. With cigarettes being made by the mile and pipe tobacco by the ton, the company was also the largest manufacturer of cigars in the country.

Employees benefited from subsidised canteens and surgeries offering medical, dental and chiropody treatment as well as a sports ground opposite the factory.

The factory closed in 1986 and most of the buildings were demolished and replaced with housing. This modern photograph shows the grade II listed former administration block, now known as the Wills Building, which was converted into 114 apartments.

Photo: Tom Yellowley.

The Wills Tobacco factory in 1965.

Benton Hall

This substantial three-storey mansion, pictured in around 1900, was built in about 1760 for Thomas Bigge, a member of a prominent local family with business interests in land, collieries and banking. The building stood within a 30-acre estate that lay to the east of what is now Red Hall Drive, close to the Coast Road and clearly marked as Little Benton House on the first edition of the Ordnance Survey map 1858. Confusingly, an elder brother of Thomas had already built for himself an impressive residence at Benton Front Street, which he named Benton House.

William Losh, founder of the Walker Iron Works, acquired Little Benton House in 1822, changed its name to Benton White Hall and lived there for at least 20 years.

The estate was converted into botanical gardens and opened to the public during the Whitsun Bank Holiday weekend of 1854, when an estimated 7,000 visitors attended the event. Special cheap trains ran from Tynemouth, North Shields and Newcastle to Walker station, which was described as 'within a few minutes' walk of the gardens'. Horse-drawn omnibuses ran directly to the gardens from Barras Bridge. For an admission charge of 6d (half price for children} visitors could enjoy conservatories, lawns, parterres, sculptures, brass bands, archery contests and a firework display at dusk. On one occasion a Montgolfier balloon ascent was the main attraction. However, a proposed Zoological section never materialised.

From around the late 1850s the property and grounds belonged to John Anthony Woods, a Newcastle banker with business connections to the coal and timber trade, who renamed it Benton Hall. At the 1871 census Woods was living there with his wife, six children, a governess and 15 servants. Benton Hall became vacant from around 1900 and remained unoccupied until about 1929 after which it was demolished. The debris, plus a quantity of earth, was used to infill the 70ft deep quarry on Newton Road, in preparation for its use by Heaton Stannington Football Club. The former Benton Hall estate was later transformed into a residential estate that contained the Lochside pub, approximately on the site of the earlier mansion.

Benton Hall c1900.

Benton Park

Benton Park was another significant 18th century mansion in extensive grounds. It was opposite Benton Hall on the other side of the country lane now known as Red Hall Drive. At one time Benton Park was called the Red Hall. Around 1870 a directory records that 'the mansion enjoys a beautiful situation commanding fine views of Gateshead Fell and the North Shields railway.

Benton Park is clearly shown on the second edition of the 1890 Ordnance Survey map. The site is now covered by Benton Hall Walk and adjoining streets.

Benton Park, with its projecting wings linked to the main block by curving walls or arcades was designed around 1780 for William Brown, a colliery owner. Later owners included other coal owners or their agents. In the late 1860s it belonged to Edward Liddell, a corn merchant who lived there with his wife, son, brother, sister and 10 servants comprising a butler, footman, housekeeper, cook, laundress, sewing maid and four housemaids. Liddell's wife was a daughter of Richard Grainger, who redeveloped central Newcastle in the mid-19th century, and her name, along with those of her 12 brothers and sisters, is remembered in some of her father's new streets in Elswick.

The surrounding estate was also home to a herd of deer. In 1854 a man with two dogs was arrested at night for poaching and was imprisoned.

Following several years of non-occupation in the early 1900s, part of the estate was sold in 1913 for an extension to Byker and Heaton cemetery, which had opened in 1890. The mansion was demolished in the 1930s and the remainder of the estate was sold to make way for Cochrane Park.

Attached to the north side of the estate was Benton Park Farm, whose main access was from Dark Lane, since renamed Etherstone Avenue. Lord Armstrong's land in north Northumberland included the historic Adderstone Hall near Belford and it would now seem that Etherstone Avenue in High Heaton was probably made synonymous with Adderstone Crescent in Jesmond as a result of the old Northumbrian name for an adder being ether.

The second edition of the 1890 Ordnance Survey map shows the location of Benton Park.

The Lochside

Cochrane Park's only pub opened on Red Hall drive in 1954 on the site of Benton Hall. It was named after the coastal steamer that carried beer from James Deuchar's Montrose brewery in Scotland to Tyneside. According to some drinkers the beer tasted even better after a stormy 16-hour sea voyage.

Bobby Mitchell, the former Newcastle United and Scottish international left winger, was landlord for several years until his death in 1993. In Mitchell's 12-year career at Newcastle he made 410 appearances, scored 113 goals and won three FA Cup winners medals.

The image shows the pub in 1966 – note the blue star sign featuring the coastal steamer.

The Lochside steamer was launched in 1905 and gave the pub its name. The ship was renamed the Helmsman in 1925 and reported missing in 1927.

The Lochside Pub in 1966.

Henderson Hall

Initially known as the New Hall, this first hall of residence for men studying at Armstrong College (now part of Newcastle University) was opened in 1932 by Viscount Grey, president of the college, on land donated by Sir Cecil A Cochrane at Etherstone Avenue, adjacent to his earlier sports ground.

Three years later the building was renamed Henderson Hall after George Edward Henderson (1844-1937), a member of the College Council, who had provided £50,000 for its construction, initially as an anonymous gift. Henderson, the son of a timber merchant with family connections to the coal trade, began work in a Quayside office before joining the Newcastle and Gateshead Water Company, eventually becoming a director and its chairman.

Henderson had many business interests, including directorships of local companies, and devoted much of his leisure to local educational and other institutions. He was regarded as one of the North East's greatest philanthropists. His many gifts included the funding of St Nicholas' Cathedral's library, the completion of St Luke's Parish Church at Spital Tongues and the extension to St Michael's Parish Church at Byker. To mark his 90th birthday, Henderson gifted his large art collection to the Laing Art Gallery. He bequeathed one million pounds to be divided between Armstrong College, the Medical School and the Royal Victoria Infirmary.

The three-sided double-storey building with its large hipped and dormered roof (containing attics) is arranged around a central lawn together with a brick wall on the fourth side, divided by a pair of ornamental wrought iron gates. The building contained 79 bed-sits with built-in wardrobes and washbasins in each room plus accommodation for a warden and five members of the academic staff. Student accommodation cost £65 per year. Although it was hoped three similar halls of residence would be built nearby this never happened.

Around 30 years later additional accommodation was built close by but these three- and five-storey rectangular brick buildings have now been demolished as surplus to requirements and are due to be replaced by a new sports complex. Henderson Hall, photographed here in 1985, is no longer in use and, although protected as a Grade II listed structure, its future had yet to be decided. However in June 2023, the hall was seriously damaged in a fire.

Henderson Hall in 1985 and, inset, one of the sparse students' rooms from that year. Sadly, the hall was seriously damaged by a fire on 8 June, 2023 (inset left, photo credit: Colin Pearce).

BENTON

Introduction

The area to the north of High Heaton and Cochrane Park, up to and including Benton Park Road, Four Lane Ends and Benton Front Street is defined, in this book, as Benton. Benton first appeared in records in 1190 as 'Bentune' indicating it was probably a farm or settlement where beans were grown.

While some sources today describe Benton Front Street as Benton Village, others refer to it as Longbenton Village. This confusion seems to stem from a time when the large parish of Longbenton, covering around 9,000 acres, consisted of five townships of which Benton was the largest. It was referred to as Long Benton to distinguish it from the nearby smaller township of Little Benton. The other three townships were Weetslade, Killingworth and Walker. Weetslade included Seaton Burn, Dudley, Annitsford, Wideopen and part of Hazlerigg. In more recent times, North Tyneside Council have addressed the problem by putting up 'Welcome to Benton' road signs at either end of Front Street.

According to one local historian in 1821, the township of Benton covered around 3,000 acres, had a population of about 1,500 and consisted of 'one long street built upon a rock and is dry, pleasant and healthy'. It contained four farmsteads, three public houses (three remain) and a boarding school. Longbenton colliery, of which the William (Billy) pit formed part, belonged to Matthew Bell, Richard Bell and Dixon Brown. The church, dedicated to St Bartholomew, stood around half a mile north east from the village. This sketch dates from around 1890.

In 1765 Benton village felt 'a violent shock like that of an earthquake' which 'disjointed all the stone houses' and 'inhabitants fled into the fields'. One gentleman's garden and some fields sank by more than two feet. At the time collieries left as much coal underground as had been removed, in order to support land and buildings above ground. Because of high demand from London for High Main coal, these supporting pillars of coal were removed and replaced with timber props that were not strong enough. As a result, rock measuring 'two miles square by 75 fathoms (450 feet) thick' collapsed into old coal workings. Fortunately, no one was killed.

Around ten years earlier, Charles Hutton, the youngest son of a colliery supervisor, had spent a short time working at Old Longbenton Colliery. A childhood accident meant he could not continue working as a hewer. He had had a good education, particularly in mathematics, so he became a teacher, firstly in Jesmond and then in Newcastle. Before 1770 he was employed by Newcastle Corporation to make a survey and then a map of Newcastle and Gateshead, which is one of the earliest and most reliable plans of both towns. Hutton was appointed Professor of Mathematics at the Royal Military Academy, Woolwich. In 1774 he became a Fellow of the Royal Society. He gained a national reputation as a distinguished mathematician and prolific writer. He died in 1823 aged 85. A street in Newcastle, leading off Sandyford Road, is named Hutton Terrace.

The west end of Front Street Benton and, inset, an early sketch of how Benton village used to look.

Benton Grange

Very little is known about Benton Grange, which stood at the western end of what is now called Benton Park Road. The property was probably built for Matthew Liddell, manager of the nearby South Gosforth colliery that opened in 1829 with a subterranean ball at a depth of 1,000 feet. A few hundred people danced to the music of the Coxlodge brass band to celebrate the winning of the High Main seam of coal, a difficult and expensive process due to the Ninety Fathom Dyke, a geological fault.

Following the sale of South Gosforth colliery by the Brandling family to John Bowes in the early 1850s, Benton Grange became the home of George Foreman, who ran a drapery business specialising in funeral attire at Grey Street in Newcastle. He lived at Benton Grange for 30 years.

In 1887 the Roman Catholic Church considered acquiring the property for the residence of the Bishop of Hexham and Newcastle, but the following year it was decided to convert the buildings into a home for penitent girls to be run by the Convent of the Good Shepherd. At the 1891 census 34 women lived there, most of whom were single and described as laundresses. The laundry (now demolished) was opposite the convent on the other side of the main road, It was known locally as the Laundry Road before being officially named Benton Park Road.

Benton Grange closed in 1984 following the sale of some land in the 1970s to St Mary's Catholic School. The building was used as student accommodation until it was demolished in 1987. It was replaced by The Cloisters residential estate. The headstones belonging to the convent's private burial ground were replaced by a single memorial stone inscribed 'Pray for the repose of the souls of the 48 Good Shepherd sisters and their Chaplain who lie buried here' No known photograph of the building exists. Instead, the position of the property and surrounding area is shown on this copy of the 1898 Ordnance Survey map.

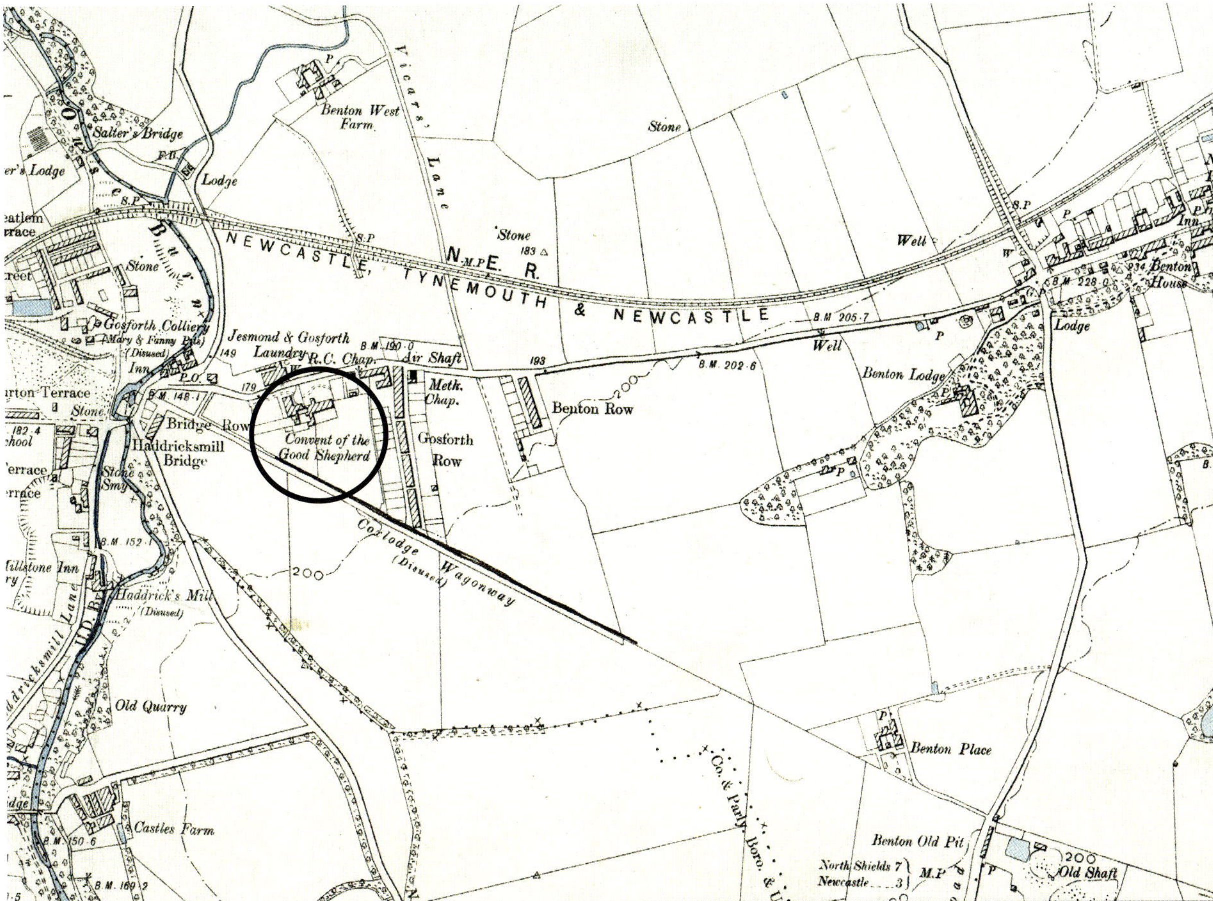

An 1898 map showing Benton Grange which by this time was The Convent of the Good Shepherd.

St Mary's School

St Mary's Catholic School settled at Benton Park Road in 1966 as a technical school for boys, having transferred from Westmorland Road in Newcastle where it had been since 1954. This photograph of the school is dated 1969. In 1977 the school became a co-educational Catholic comprehensive along with two other similar schools until they merged on this site in completely new school buildings in 2011, forming the only Catholic co-educational secondary school in the city. The school caters for around 1,000 students and gained Academy status in 2013.

The school was built over the approximate site of Gosforth Row, a long street of back-to-back low-rise cottages erected in the early 1830s by the nearby South Gosforth colliery for their miners. Close by was another shorter row of miners' cottages, Benton Row, which has been replaced by the Haversham Close residential estate. At the 1891 census, both rows had a combined population of 637 people living in 132 cottages, In almost all cases each household contained at least one coal miner. Living conditions in both rows were described as bad or evil, with uneven brick floors, a ladder to the upper storey bedroom, which had no ceiling, no sanitation and the nearest water supply nearly half a mile away. There were 'noisome ash heaps' in the area and, not surprisingly, a prevalence of scarlet fever.

Adjoining Gosforth Row and fronting the turnpike road (now Benton Park Road) was a New Connexion Methodist Chapel, probably built around the early 1830s and now used as a car repair workshop. The sketch, drawn around 1865, illustrates what is assumed to be Gosforth Row with the taller Methodist Chapel at the far end. Almost opposite the Methodist Chapel is a row of 10 brick terraced cottages, built in 1913/14 by the Northumberland Aged Mineworkers' Homes Association for retired pitmen. This type of home was provided throughout the Northumberland and Durham coalfield from around 1900, partially funded by deductions from miners' wages.

St Mary's Catholic School settled at Benton Park Road in 1966. Here's it is in 1969. Opposite page: The sketch of miners' cottages in what is assumed to be Gosforth Row is dated c1865 and the stone plaque can be seen on the row of Aged Mineworkers Homes on the opposite side of Benton Park Road.

Benton Park View

In 1946 the Government purchased around 50 acres of farmland between Benton Park Road and the former Coxlodge Waggonway for the headquarters of their new Ministry of Pensions and National Insurance department, which was due to open two years later as part of the National Health Service.

The complex eventually consisted mainly of single-storey brick buildings arranged in H shaped blocks, intended to be a temporary solution until something more permanent could be built. In fact, they remained in use as offices for over 50 years. The buildings were designed so that in the event of another war, a distinct possibility at the time, they could be quickly converted into emergency hospital accommodation for service personnel. King George VI officially opened the complex. From the 1960s several taller office blocks were added.

Widely known as 'the ministry' by the 1970s the site employed around 10,000 staff. Facilities included a bank, post office, gents' hairdresser, garden shop, canteen and licensed bar. Buses for employees ran to most parts of the region. This 1996 photograph features some of the 1960s office blocks alongside Benton Park Road, now replaced by housing around a street named 'Ministry Close'.

At the beginning of the 21st century the site was completely reorganised. Most of the buildings were demolished and replaced with 16 grey metal and glass structures including 11 multi-storey office blocks named after Northumbrian castles. The five single-storey buildings included two restaurants, the Amble Inn and the Wark Inn, and a nursery. Extensive car parks and private housing now occupy the rest of the site.

This multi-agency site, now known as Benton Park View is mainly occupied by Her Majesty's Revenue and Customs (HMRC) and the Department for Work and Pensions (DWP) as well as other departments such as the Health and Safety Executive and the Pension, Disability and Carers Service. It is now one of the largest secure civilian government complexes in Europe.

Opposite page: An aerial view from 1970 showing the headquarters of the Ministry of Pensions and National Insurance department and, inset, the building in 1996.

Freeman Hospital
Coxlodge Waggonway
Benton Park Road
Metro Railway

Longbenton Metro Station

Known locally as the 'Ministry Halt' and officially as Longbenton Halt, this basic station with two platforms and a restricted weekday-only service opened in 1947 in Lealholm Road, a residential thoroughfare accessed from Benton Park Road, opposite the Ministry of Pensions and National Insurance complex. The station was built specifically to cater for the huge number of employees expected to work at the site. The rail track, over 80 years old at the time, had been laid by the former Blyth & Tyne Railway for their popular service between Newcastle and Tynemouth.

Longbenton station reopened in 1980, after some modifications, as part of the first section of Tyne & Wear's new Metro system between Newcastle's Haymarket and Tynemouth – Britain's first rapid light transit system. The station was largely rebuilt in 1999.

Also in 1980, at nearby Four Lane Ends a Metro Interchange with bus and car parking facilities opened on the site of the former Long Benton station operated by the Blyth & Tyne Railway between 1864 and 1871. Long Benton station was replaced in 1871 by the more convenient Benton Station, a short distance away on what is now called Station Road. This became part of the Metro system in 1980.

Photo: John Mann.

Opposite page: A rundown Longbenton Station in 1969 and, above, the Metro station in 2023.

Benton Lodge

The Victorian residence called Benton Lodge appears to have been built in the mid-1840s for William Smith, the shipbuilder, who, until then, had been living at Benton House on Benton Front Street. The new building stood in several acres of woodland, surrounded by fields, close to the site of today's Benton Lodge Avenue. In 1851 Smith was living here with his wife, sister-in-law and seven servants. At this time, he was described as a merchant shipowner, shipbuilder and farmer of 31 acres employing one agricultural labourer. Smith's shipyard at St Peter's in Byker was the forerunner of Smith's Dock at North Shields, which, in the early 1900s was the world's largest ship-repairing business with all the major oil companies in the world as regular customers.

Following Smith's death in 1860 the property was occupied for over 30 years by various members of the Anderson family of colliery owners, land owners and solicitors.

The next occupants were the Hiddleston family of tailors and woollen merchants. In the 1930s their name was used for one of the streets that replaced Benton Lodge Estate – Hiddleston Avenue.

One of the last residents before the house was demolished in the early 1930s was Sir Archibald Ross (1867-1931), the pioneering marine engineer who spent his working life at R & W Hawthorn Leslie's St Peter's Works. The four small stained-glass windows in the crypt of Newcastle's St Nicholas' Cathedral were donated by his family in his memory and feature aspects of his life such as industry, music and fishing.

This aerial view, dating from the early to mid-1930s shows Benton Lodge in its sprawling, largely wooded estate surrounded by housing: Swarland Avenue and The Crescent (top), Hiddleston Avenue (right), Benton Park Road (bottom) and Benton Lodge Avenue (left).

A 1930s aerial view showing Benton Lodge inside its large wooded estate.

Sutherland Park

The Old Novocastrians Rugby Football Club (Old Novos – now just Novos) was founded in 1899 for former pupils of Newcastle's Royal Grammar School who wished to continue playing rugby. The term Novocastrian describes anyone born in Newcastle. Until 1925, when a 9-acre field adjoining the Benton Lodge Estate became available, the club was nomadic as it did not have its own ground.

Sir Arthur Munro Sutherland, a former pupil at the school and a major benefactor to both Newcastle and the school, was involved in the negotiations to purchase the field as a permanent home for the club. Sutherland, the owner of a local steamship company and former Lord Mayor of Newcastle, bought the land for £4,000 and engaged local architects Marshall and Tweedy to design the pavilion, which opened in 1928, and improve the layout of the ground, which was to include tennis courts. The ground was later named Sutherland Park.

At present the club has several teams, including one for women, that play in various local leagues and a playing membership of well over 400.

Sutherland Park in 2023.

The Pavilion at Sutherland Park in 1928.

Novocastrians RFC

Manor Park School

Manor Park Secondary Technical School for Boys opened in 1960 at Benton Road between the Fairways Estate and the Coxlodge waggonway, on land previously used as a golf course. The intention was to amalgamate two older schools, Heaton Technical in North Heaton and Middle Street Commercial in Walker, with the aim of raising standards to grammar school level and feeding the colleges of further education. School buildings consisted of a four-storey central block flanked by structures containing classrooms or workshops with a large playground to the rear and a sports field beyond. Pupil numbers were expected to reach 850, including sixth form students. The photograph is dated 1966.

From 1967 the school turned comprehensive and in 1983 it merged with Heaton School on Newton Road because of fewer pupils and government cut backs. It was known as Heaton Manor School, although the two schools still operated on separate sites. In 2004 the school moved to a new enlarged site at Newton Road and the Benton Road buildings were demolished and replaced with the Manor Park residential development.

Former pupils include Jimmy Nail, actor, singer-songwriter and star of TV's Auf Wiedersehen Pet, and Dennis Tueart, England International footballer, who helped Sunderland win the FA Cup in 1973.

Manor Park Secondary Technical School for Boys in 1966.

Edwardian Manor House

This recent photograph features the impressive Edwardian mansion, known as the Manor House and now part of Northumbria University's campus at Coach Lane. The mansion was built in rural Benton for Arthur J Haggie, a member of the family of ropemakers, to accommodate his expanding family of seven children and several servants. Arthur was the twelfth and last child of Robert Hood Haggie, who founded the ropeworks in 1843.

In around 1905 Arthur and his family moved from Willington Villa, adjoining the ropeworks to their new home at Benton, which was surrounded by open countryside with a small lake. Apart from ropemaking, Arthur had business interests in greenhouses and a cabinet maker's workshop. He served as a Northumberland County Council Alderman and was a county magistrate for nearly 40 years. He lived at Benton until he died in 1941 aged 84.

This Edwardian mansion, known as the Manor House, is now part the university campus at Coach Lane.

Benton Barrage Balloon Station

During the Second World War the RAF made extensive use of barrage balloons as a defensive measure against low flying enemy aircraft such as dive-bombers. Eventually there were a few thousand barrage balloon sites in the UK, usually around strategic targets and generally operated by the Women's Auxiliary Air Force.

One of these sites was at Benton in an area now occupied by Newcastle University's sports ground at the top end of Coach Lane. The Benton barrage balloon station dealt primarily with the collection and repair of damaged balloons and tethering cables from sites on Tyneside. The balloon hangar, pictured in 1992, where balloons were inflated for testing has been demolished along with other related buildings.

Steel cables, up to one mile long, were suspended from the balloons and a few balloons would create a mesh of steel to protect a strategic target. Enemy aircraft would be forced to fly high, resulting in less accurate bombing, more effective anti-aircraft fire and more active defending aircraft. Eventually explosive devices were fitted to the tethering cables, meaning destruction of any aircraft, friend or foe, involved in a collision or firing its guns at the balloon.

Balloons were made from a silvery synthetic material, filled with hydrogen. The gas needed topping up daily. Around 60 feet long and 25 feet in diameter, the balloons were tethered to concrete blocks or specialised vehicles and raised or lowered by winches.

Left: Benton Barrage Balloon Station in 1992, just before it was demolished. Above: A barrage balloon at Silver Lonnen

Barrage balloon crew relaxing in Heaton Park in 1941.

Benton House

William Bigge, an Essex lawyer, moved to Newcastle in 1666 to marry into the wealthy Dent family. His marriage settlement included various estates in the Tyneside area. Some of Bigge's descendants served as High Sheriff of Northumberland, Mayor of Newcastle and Private Secretary to royalty. One of Northumberland's most notable merchant and banking families, for over 70 years they also owned the colliery at Wallsend known as Bigges Main.

In the 1740s William's grandson, another William, had a two-storey house, Benton House, built for himself on Benton Front Street. Around 30 years later the house was substantially altered to include a fashionable classical-style façade overlooking several acres of parkland, which meant the house entrance was moved from the north to the south side of the building.

In 1803 the Bigge family moved to another part of Northumberland. Later occupants of Benton House included the Smith family of shipbuilders whose business developed into the world-famous Smith's Dock Company. In the early 1900s the house was converted into a club house for the Benton Park Golf Club. Founded in 1909, the 18-hole course occupied the former private parkland that reached as far south as the Coxlodge Waggonway.

During the late 1940s Newcastle City Council compulsorily purchased the golf course for housing and a school. The housing estate was named the Fairways Estate and most of the street names had a golfing connection, including Muirfield Road, Dunlop Close and Gleneagles Close. The school was called Manor Park.

When the golf club relocated to Arcot Hall near Cramlington, the Benton Conservative Club took over and continue to occupy Benton House. The house and the Ha-Ha in the adjoining garden are Grade II listed structures. A Ha-Ha is a vertical drop or ditch, usually between a house and parkland, that controls livestock without affecting the view. The Ha-Ha is now screened by shrubs for safety reasons. Access to Benton House is by Hoylake Avenue.

Opposite page: This modern photo of Benton House clearly shows the Ha-Ha in front of the building, now screened by shrubs and bushes for safety reasons.

Georgian Manor House and Horse Gin

Adjoining the busy road junction at Four Lane Ends is a two-storey stone building with a steeply pitched roof. It originated as a farmhouse in the mid-1700s and became known as the Manor House. In 1983 the house and its associated buildings were converted into flats in a partially enclosed area named Teal Close. The word 'manor' originally meant a unit of land and not necessarily a building.

At the rear is an open sided circular structure with a conical roof, known as a horse gin or gin-gan(g), which would have been the powerhouse for threshing grain. Horses were harnessed to a large horizontal wheel under the conical roof. When they walked around the circle they turned the wheel, which used cogs, gears and beams to activate a threshing machine in the adjacent barn. The word 'gin' is derived from engine and 'gan' stems from the local dialect word for to go. The machinery became obsolete following the introduction of steam power and no longer exists, but the circular structure and the Manor House are Grade II listed.

From the late 1920s a residential estate, with streets such as Manor Road, Manor Drive and Manor Walk, was built on open farmland south of the Manor House.

Photographed in 2018, the former Georgian Manor House near Four Lane Ends and, opposite page, the intricate timber-work inside the horse gin's conical roof.

Benton Ale House

A short distance from Four Lane Ends on Benton Front Street is the former Sun Inn, pictured here in 1987. The pub's name was changed to the Benton Ale House by Wolverhampton and Dudley Breweries (Marstons from 2007) following their acquisition of Cameron's Hartlepool Brewery in 1992.

The pub probably opened on this site around the mid-1700s as coal mining developed in the vicinity.

The Benton Ale House in 2023.

Former Coach House and West Wing of Benton House

Immediately opposite the Benton Ale House is the former coach house once belonging to Benton House. This single-storey sandstone building with a pitched slate roof, small turret and weathervane is now a restaurant.

A little further east along Front Street, almost opposite the Black Bull Inn, is a classical-style two-storey stone building with a shop at ground level. It is part of the north side of Benton House (the main section of which faces south) and dates from around 1900 when the west wing was rebuilt. Features include a pediment overlooking Front Street containing a circular keyed window, or oculus, that is repeated on the south side of this Grade II listed building.

The classical-style west wing of Benton House facing Front Street. Opposite page: The former coach house, now a restaurant, also on Front Street.

Black Bull Inn

The two-storey building to the right of this photograph of a section of Benton Front Street in 1936, is part of the earlier Black Bull Inn. Traditionally this inn is believed to be the oldest of the area's three pubs, dating back to the mid-1700s when coal mining was becoming an important activity in this district. Set back slightly from the road, the Black Bull was an active coaching inn with stables at the rear, including one for the local vicar whose vicarage stood nearby.

In 1938 the present Black Bull Inn replaced the earlier building. Later the old cottages to the left of the pub were demolished to make way for a car park.

The single deck tram is travelling east towards the terminus at Forest Hall, having just left Four Lane Ends, which is barely visible on the left.

A tram approaches the Black Bull in 1936.

The original Black Bull Inn. Note the insurance plaque on the wall guaranteeing premiums paid to date.

The present Black Bull in 1966.

Benton Former Vicarage

When this vicarage in Benton village opened in 1734 it had probably been expected that the old, dilapidated medieval Parish Church of St Andrew, around half a mile away towards Forest Hall, would have been rebuilt in the village. This never happened, probably because the rocky ground of the village would have been unsuitable for a burial ground. Instead, the church was rebuilt on its original foundations and renamed St Bartholomew's.

The vicar who was living here in the 1880s with his wife, daughter and three servants had the appropriate name of Oliver Churchyard.

Costing around £400, this two-storey stone-built vicarage, now Grade II listed, was taken over in 1950 by the Ethel Williams Halls of Residence for female university students. Dr Ethel Williams (1863-1948) had been an active suffragist, pacifist and social welfare campaigner. In 1906 she became Newcastle's first female general medical practitioner. She was the first woman in Newcastle to hold a driving licence and allegedly the first to be seen driving a car in the north of England. In 2018 a plaque was unveiled at 3 Osborne Terrace, Jesmond, where she lived and worked from 1910 to 1924.

In 2000, no longer needed for student accommodation the vicarage was converted into private apartments. The present vicarage is nearer the church in Station Road.

The Grade II listed, stone-built former vicarage, now converted into private apartments.

North House

North House is the next substantial property east of the former vicarage and overlooks the junction with Coach Lane. This two-storey stone-built house has a Georgian central doorway with a broken pediment over Tuscan columns, dates from the mid- to late 1700s and is Grade II Listed. The photograph was taken in 2017. Henry Eagle, who lived here during and for a short while after the First World War, was the inventor of Iglodine, an antiseptic. The Iglodine Company was at the lower end of Pilgrim Street. Originally called Heinrich Igel, Eagle came to Tyneside from his native Romania in 1881 at the age of 19. He worked as a chemist for a number of years.

The name Iglodine is a combination of Igel and iodine, its main chemical component. It was the most lucrative of his many inventions, which ranged from cosmetics to engraving machines. Often described as one of the North East's most colourful characters, Eagle led a lavish lifestyle, often hosting a 'crowded international dinner table'. While relaxing at home he often wore knee-breeches and a fez.

From around 1950 North House was taken over by Ethel Williams Hall until it was converted into private apartments. Behind North House is the Williams Park residential estate.

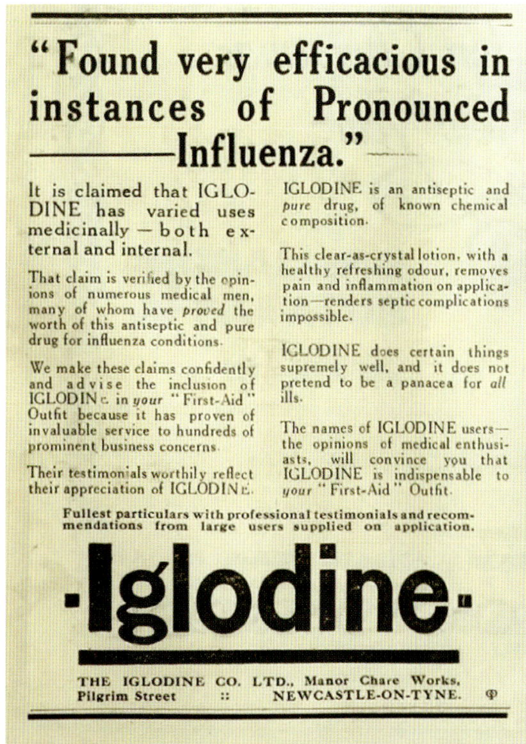

Iglodine's premises on Pilgrim Street in 1928 and an advert for their product.

North House in 2017. It is now private appartments.

Toll Gate

Coach Lane had once been subject to a toll of a penny for pedestrians and 3d for carts. The tollhouse and gate were at the junction with Front Street which later became a Police House - note the 'Police' sign above the door.

Photo: North Tyneside Libraries.

St Aidan's Catholic Church

At the top end of Coach Lane near the junction with Front Street is St Aidan's Catholic Church. It is easily missed because it was built behind a two-storey stone villa on Coach Lane and is partially screened by shrubs and trees.

Today's church was initially designed as a church hall by architect David Brown in 1963. The intention was to build the church at a later date. This never happened and the church hall was converted into the church with some alterations before it was consecrated in 1990.

Founded in 1906 in an area previously served by the Dominicans at Shieldfield, the first church building at this site was a temporary corrugated iron structure, known as a tin church, that lasted for many years.

St Aiden's in 2023. The church are the buildings to the right of the photograph.

The Ship Inn

The present Ship Inn, which opened in 1904 is the tall building with the gabled roof as seen from the east end of Benton Front Street and pictured here a year later. This highly detailed brick building has some attractive stone features and decorated rainwater hoppers.

On the far side of the pub is the original, smaller Ship Inn, converted into flats after 1904 and now a restaurant.

Behind the trees on the opposite side of the road was Benton Farm, now replaced by the Manorfields residential development and a car showroom.

The Ship Inn in 1905 and, opposite page, a modern photograph of the pub.

Benton National School

The first building in Benton to include a schoolroom, apart from the parish church, was Church House (now demolished) opposite the main gates of the church. In 1669 the parish clerk doubled up as the schoolmaster as a way of saving money.

Around a century later, the parish clerk, Thomas Rutter, who lived in Benton Village opposite the Ship Inn, was given the position of schoolmaster and his home became Rutter's School. He taught boys on the ground floor while his wife taught girls on the floor above with access from an outside wooden staircase. Two boys from the school, Thomas Addison (1795-1860) and Robert Stephenson (1803-1859) later achieved international recognition.

Thomas Addison, the second son of the village grocer whose home and shop stood opposite the Black Bull Inn became Senior Physician to Guy's Hospital in London and identified the medical condition known as Addison's Disease. He presented a stained-glass window to St Bartholomew's church in memory of his parents.

Robert Stephenson, the civil engineer and only son of George Stephenson, the railway pioneer, is said to have travelled to school from his home at Dial Cottage, Killingworth on a donkey, occasionally carrying mining tools that needed sharpening at Benton Smithy.

Benton National School opened in 1871 on a site next to the former Rutter's school, which was then demolished. The school, which cost £1,120 catered for 200 children in two classrooms, separated by one large room. In 1899 another large room, a smaller room and a cloakroom were added. Classrooms were heated by either a coke stove or open fire. There was no running hot water and toilets were on the far side of the playground. On wintry days children often took turns at sitting near the stove.

Writing was taught by drill; 'every left elbow should be on the desk with every face turned to the right'. Young pupils used slates before progressing to pen and ink. Arithmetic and tables were taught by rote. Truancy was a constant problem and the headmaster personally searched for absentees in the village, except during harvest time when he allegedly turned a blind eye. Medals were awarded to pupils who had never been absent.

This image of the school on Front Street is dated around 1890 and following the opening of a new school in the area during 1970 for five to nine-year-olds the building was demolished three years later. St Bartholomews Court residential development now more than covers the school site. Gate pillars inscribed 'Boys' and 'Girls' with part of the school's boundary wall have survived.

Photo: North Tyneside Libraries.

Benton National School and, below, all that is left of the site are the gate pillars inscribed 'boys' and 'girls'.

William (or Billy) Pit

The William Pit, or Billy Pit as it was more generally known, owned by the Willington Colliery, opened in around 1808, a few hundred yards south of the Front Street/Station Road junction. Before the introduction of cages miners would have descended 500 feet to the High Main coal seam either in a wicker basket or by clinging to a rope or chain. Horses were lowered in harnesses. The pit closed in 1843 although the shaft was retained for ventilation. It was gradually infilled and finally capped with concrete in 1970. Corver Way and Colliery Close residential development now cover the approximate site of the pit. A corver was a contractor who supplied and maintained corves or baskets made of hazel, which were used to transport coal before the introduction of tubs.

Most mining families lived at the pithead in small, terraced cottages without basic facilities. Each cottage consisted of a living room and a scullery, both with stone floors partially covered by 'clippy' mats. A wooden ladder led to the bedroom, the only room in the attic. The low roof made it necessary to crawl into bed. Water had to be carried from a nearby well, paraffin oil was used for lighting but at least coal for the living room fire was free and plentiful. A rain-water barrel with the top sawn off served as a bath. People usually bathed in the pantry where there was some privacy, Detached allotments were provided for growing vegetables and there was a communal piggery.

At the time of the 1841 census there were 23 dwellings housing 131 people, 52 of whom worked at the pit. Pit workers' ages ranged from seven to 70. Surprisingly one 15-year-old girl was described as a 'coal miner'. Overcrowding must have been a major problem, when, for example 13 people lived in one cottage with 11 in each of two others. The situation may have been eased by shift work when some beds were in constant use.

For several years after the pit closed the cottages were occupied by workers at Benton Quarry. In the early 1900s two outside water taps were installed to serve the community, but without drains, sinks or toilet facilities, the cottages were condemned in 1936 and demolished some time later.

These photographs show the front and back of Billy Pit Cottages a few years before demolition.

The old pit shaft and, opposite page, the Billy Pit Cottages in 1936.

Benton Parish Church

Benton Parish Church at Station Road was dedicated to St Bartholomew in 1791 following a major rebuild on the same site as the 12th century parish Church of St Andrew, which 'has long been in a very decayed and ruinous state and condition'. St Andrew's Church was originally built to serve the extensive medieval parish of Longbenton, midway between its two principal townships of Benton and Killingworth. Other townships in the parish were Little Benton, Weetslade and Walker.

In 1340 the church of St Andrew and some land belonging to the parish were gifted to Balliol College, Oxford to 'sustain six scholars and a chaplain'. This endowment continues to the present day and the name Balliol frequently occurs in the area. The Balliol family once owned land in the north of England and John Balliol became King of Scots in the late 1200s.

William Newton, a prominent Newcastle architect designed the new church in around 1790 on the foundations of the original church but without the chancel, which was the responsibility of Balliol College. Following the theft of lead from the roof of the medieval chancel in the 1850s, the Balliol family provided the present chancel, which cost £202. In 1874 the church underwent a major restoration and a south aisle was added to an otherwise aisle-less nave. A battlemented porch was added in 1885, a new vestry was built in 1888 and the octagonal church hall dates from 1980.

Nothing has survived from the original church of St Andrew apart from a few grave slabs and ledger stones. The only remaining parts of Newton's church are the north wall of the nave and the battlemented tower with pinnacles at each corner, topped by a short spire.

St Bartholomew's churchyard contains the burial places of two Tyneside shipbuilders - Charles Mitchell of Low Walker and his brother-in-law Charles Sheriton Swan, founder of the firm that became Swan Hunter and Wigham Richardson at Wallsend.

St Bartholomew's in 2023. Opposite page. The interior of the church in 1938 and the exterior in the 1920s.

Benton Square

Benton Square was a large square of humble cottages built in around the1760s by the recently opened East Longbenton Colliery for their employees' families. This new colliery opened specifically to replace the flooded West Longbenton Colliery in what is now High Heaton, alongside the Coxlodge Waggonway near the Newton Park Hotel on Benton Road.

Each of the cottages is thought to have consisted of just one room, together with an attic that served as a bedroom, accessed by a ladder – notice the roof vents on the photograph. The cramped conditions may have been eased by shift work which often resulted in some beds being continually occupied. An open fire used miners' free coal allowance for cooking and heating, and the houses were lit by oil lamps. There was no indoor plumbing and neighbours shared the limited outdoor facilities that were available. Colliery cottages were often poorly constructed because they were built too quickly, sometimes on land that was badly drained or otherwise unsuitable but because they were provided rent-free, families had little choice but to remain.

The best known of the colliery's pits was the Prosperous Pit, where in 1772 engineer John Smeaton built a pumping engine and, five years later a 'water coal gin', which could raise coal from a depth of 500 feet, replacing the work of four men and 16 horses.

The East Longbenton Colliery was served by the Killingworth Waggonway where George Stephenson introduced his standard 4ft 8-and-a-half-inch gauge, now used by most railways worldwide. Part of this waggonway can now be used by pedestrians, cyclists and horse riders.

The site of the colliery dwellings and colliery are now occupied by an industrial estate close to the Asda hypermarket on Whitley Road. In Wesley drive is a Primitive Methodist chapel, built in 1904 to replace an earlier chapel on the same site dating from 1833. The present chapel continued in use until 1977 and is now commercial premises. There may also have been an 18th century inn or tavern that developed into today's Wheatsheaf Inn, which once operated as a coaching inn.

Opposite page: Benton Square in 1910 and, inset, the most recent chapel in 2021 is now commercial premises.

Photo: North Tyneside Libraries.

Select Bibliography

Archaeologia Aeliana (1995) (Colliery Cottages) HD Brown
Bygone High Heaton (1988) W Muir
Bygone Longbenton (2000) W G Elliott & E Smith
Parish Church of St Bartholomew (2002) W G Elliott
Coals from Newcastle (2009) L Turnbull
Cochrane Park correspondence B Durham, R Long & J Telfer
Diocesan Archivist (2003) R Gard
Family History of Haggie's Ropeworks Dr M Haggie
Gone but not forgotten The Forties (1991) B Stephenson & F Manders
Gorgeous Gosforth tour notes (1990) Newcastle City Guides
Heaton Stannington AFC (2014) K Mochrie
Heavy Nights (1995) B Bennison
Henderson Hall Booklet (undated)
Hidden Gems (2012) D Dodds
History of Wallsend (1923) W Richardson
Hospitals (1996) L Redhead
Linden Hall booklet (1982) C Baglee
Lost Houses of Newcastle and Northumberland (1996) T Faulkner & P Lowery
Newcastle & Gateshead Architecture & Heritage (2014) T Faulkner, P Beacock, P Jones, T Yellowley
Notes on Convent site (2002) J Williams
Northumberland Buildings (1992) N Pevsner
Northumberland Place Names G Watson (1970) S Beckinsall (1975)
Northumberland Family History Magazine (2003) C Eagle
Northumberland Social and Political Miscellany (1979) F Graham
Railways of Northumberland & Newcastle upon Tyne JA Wells
St Bartholomew's Church booklet Dr G W D Briggs
St Francis Church Magazine (1995)
St George's UR Church booklet (1988)
Suburban Railways of Tyneside A Young
The Great Northern Miners (2008) K & J Smith
They Played in Tyne & Wear (2010) L Pearson
Tyne & Tweed Magazine (Smiths Dock) (2001) R H Hill
Tramways of Northumberland (1961) G S Hearse
Waggonways of Northumberland (1976) C R Warn
Wheels (1980) N Hanson

Further east along Front Street, Benton, at the junction with the Manorfields Estate is a cast iron milepost indicating the distance to Newcastle and North Shields. It is still in its original position, intact, well preserved and Grade II listed. It was cast by Smith Patterson & Co at their Blaydon foundry in the late nineteenth or early twentieth century and photographed in 2017.

Back Cover: The Coast Road, 1967.

Dedicated to my dear wife Eileen (1936 - 2023)